Parties

Parties

Poems by Elizabeth Seydel Morgan

Louisiana State University Press
Baton Rouge and London
1988

Copyright © 1974, 1975, 1978, 1979, 1981, 1983, 1984, 1985, 1986, 1987, 1988 by
    Elizabeth Seydel Morgan
All rights reserved
Manufactured in the United States of America

97 96 95 94 93 92 91 90 89 88   5 4 3 2 1

Designer: Laura Roubique Gleason
Typeface: Palatino
Typesetter: Focus Graphics
Printer: Thomson-Shore, Inc.
Binder: John H. Dekker & Sons, Inc.

Library of Congress Cataloging-in-Publication Data

Morgan, Elizabeth Seydel, 1939–
      Parties : poems / by Elizabeth Seydel Morgan.
          p.   cm.
      ISBN 0-8071-1474-X (alk. paper). ISBN 0-8071-1475-8 (pbk.   :   alk.
    paper)
      I. Title.
    PS3563.0828P3   1988
    811'.54—dc 19   88-1390
                                                            CIP

Publication of this book has been supported by a grant from the National
Endowment for the Arts in Washington, D.C., a federal agency.

Some of the poems in this collection have appeared in the following publications:
*Bennington Review, Georgia Review, Greensboro Review, Iowa Review, Language, New
Virginia Review, Prairie Schooner, Richmond Quarterly, Shenandoah,* and *Virginia
Quarterly Review.*

The paper in this book meets the guidelines for permanence and durability of the
Committee on Production Guidelines for Book Longevity of the Council on Library
Resources. ∞

for Elizabeth, Matt, John

Contents

The Luncheon of the Boating Party

The Party Before the Party

The Party Before the Party

Late sun changed the bottles
to stained glass colors
on the white tablecloth
that covered the bar.

Little girls in pinafores
played tag and touch
under old locusts and Japanese maples.
They fluttered like the pattern
of shadows the breeze and the star
leaves made on the lawn.

Laughter was light, light
was light, iced drinks were light
at the party before the party.

We were lovely as children,
lingering maturely, but itchy
as children, hardly bearing
to stand so still,
ready to run and hide and seek.

I was a grownup, wearing a sundress
that left my back bare. You
came up beside me and lightly,
but with your whole hand,
touched me there.

Sex

Before she got cancer Mary Kinsella
would kiss Harvey Martin in front of us.
They'd touch and tickle in the kitchen.
We were sixteen and thought it was sickening
for a balding man and a graying lady to kiss on the lips.

I remember the night they came in
flushed from kissing in a cold car; a policeman
had caught them parked (they said "spooning" and giggled)
and made them move on.

Jim Kinsella and I were ashamed enough without that.
We'd been caught too, two frisky raccoons stopped
blackeyed in the cop's spotlight, cheek to cheek,
wet mouths opened, Jim's finger paralyzed to my nipple,
my hand stuck to the damp cloth of his crotch.
It was our first offense.

We didn't come in giggling. Sex was as serious
as death. The only thing that could make us laugh
was the question—do you think they ever do it?—
and the potbellied picture we could evoke.

But even after we hooted at it, Jim Kinsella dropped
my hand and stared at Katharine Hepburn on the drive-in's screen
and I cooled my forehead against the window and looked out
at the rows of dark cars connected by a cord.

Macho/Psyche

The macho psyche of the American
—Sam Shepard

The first word is darkeyed, muscled, moves
like a boxer—languid then quick—his black
hair springs in O's down his neck

even curls on the back of his hand
that cups the rough edge of stucco
forming the corner of shadow and light

at the square where the other one strides
in white linen, her fair hair bright in the sun,
her red patent-leather high heels flash

in syncopation with protracted castanets
while the flute note spun across the top
of the heavy air unspools into the alley

where he leans and whistles low
and though she knows where she is going
she pivots on the gritty stone.

They come together that afternoon—
strange words touching in a hushed cool room,
they lie in down and wings of sheets.

*

She lets him in, in America, helps him out
of his snow-wet coat, apologizes for her apartment,
fingers his rough plump cheeks.

In her shower he soaps her breasts, her bruise,
she giggles and clings. They sing off-key
something from Nashville or Motown

or a snatch of tune picked up at night outside
of Atlanta when he says get rid of
the spic stuff and crack me a brew

and she cuts the can with a churchkey, spews
foam that blinks like mothwings on her skin.
She cannot think for loving him.

5

At the Country Club

The lifeguard and the married lady
lap two racing lanes. They pass in crossing,
reach their ends at different times,
hang and turn and look
for the other who has looked
and dived and surfaced somewhere else.

The married lady's muscles,
lax from the hours by the babypool,
are aroused in this deep water.
She recalls her body to her,
remembers cadence, grace, and breath,
times her strokes to match the slow
and potent ones she senses
coming through the water like a pulse.

The lifeguard, sated with sun,
with fantasies the oiled young girls
and broiling days demand,
knows she matches moves
somewhere in the cool water—
tries, but can't contrive
a rhythm that will bring them
to the end of the pool together.

Shakedown Time in the Pine Forest

Past fifty feet we can't reach the seeds
even with the long steel arm
of bucket trucks,
so we come this time of year
to shake the trees.
To get more light these pines grow past
our range of picking
and their best pinecones mate up there.
The soft-scaled females suck in pollen
that hasn't sunk below the tops of trees
and the farthest from the forest floor
swell with seeds we want
to start new woods.
So we're here now in this dim place
to spread the tarps across the loam,
then ride the buckets up—each
of us beside a tree—
as far as they will go, which falls
far short of what we're here for.
My rough gloves and woolen sleeves
are not so thick
that I can't feel the furrowed bark
as I clamp the belt around it.
The generator down below
chuffs then hums and up through cables
current surges and this long trunk
I have my hands on
starts to vibrate
and all along the rows
the banded trees begin to shake,
making maybe somewhere far
from here a kind of music,
but all I hear is racket
from the blurring yellow truck
below me. Or say the sound
of shaken trees is this thick scent
of so much pine, pine bark and needle,
oil and rosin.

And now the fall, as all the cones
let loose their seeds, each seed beneath
its flicking wing. They plink and slip
against my hat, then settle
on my shoulders, stick along my sleeves.
When the air is thinned
of noise and smell, of seed and cone
and I am slowly lowered, I'll take these
with me, brush them off
on earth I've cleared at home.

At *a* Lecture

He says that *verse* derives from the verb *to turn*.
Straightforward gave us *prose*. And he goes on.

I know the curve is the sensuous line.
At L'Orangerie I slipped my fingers
past the guards to feel the rounded forms
of all the Henry Moores, to end the tension

of those artful turns. Talking in circles
is not the same as touching them. Your thigh,

your rich curls, just inches from my hand.

Daylily

The day you touched me
the first lily bloomed,
orange watered silk
cupped on the point
of a tongue.

After you'd gone
it glowed through the dusk,
closing over
its delicate pistil,
slowly folding in.

On Monday Point

We had not imagined how immense it would be
when we borrowed this clapboard house on the bay
to sleep together for the first time.

Room opens on room on room like dreams of change—
we make a game of guessing where the house will end,
which of all the beds we'll choose to lie in.

With dark, the noises start. The storm they'd warned of
back at Locust Grocery ("Big one coming up tonight")
begins by slamming distant doors.

The chimneys whine with siphoned wind.
Giant elms make leafy jabs at the gables,
something wild beats back against the ribs of the roof.

If you weren't so big I'd be afraid—
the huge house, the newness of you, noises without names,
this low cry of my own no less strange.

Island Life

Between two birches on a hill
I hang out the clothes and pretend
I'm a sailor's wife.

Because as I wrestle
the wet double sheets to the line
they remind me of sails

and when the frayed rope dips
with the weight of the sheets
I can see the boats in Casco Bay.

The big ship rounding Headlight
Point returns, I know,
from Nova Scotia.

I fork the pillowcase corners
with the knobbed wooden prongs
that came with the house

and pretend that you're a sailor.
That's why you packed this morning,
banged the door and rowed for Portland.

Now you could be at the pier with your duffle,
stuffed with the gear your woman
cleaned and folded.

You could be waiting to board the *Scotia Prince*.
You could be looking across to our island,
watching the sails of your laundry catch the wind.

Every Fact Is a Field

In the language of science, every fact is a field.
—Jacob Bronowski

It is summer on your father's farm,
South Georgia, 1956.
We are teenaged girls.

Our bare legs straddle the bare backs
of palomino quarter horses
who're nuzzling and munching clover,
the reins loose on their golden necks.

The clover is blooming, a purple field
sloping away from this knoll
to a dark stand of pines
that hides half the sun.

We're sharing a stolen cigarette,
feeling horsewarmth against our thighs,
the June air cooling on our moist skin.

We talk so long the sky draws up
the clover's color to its own field.

The horses snort, then shift.
Your leg touches mine as we watch in silence
the black pines rise,
pulling this land up and over,
taking us backward into night.

Without a word we rein our horses
and turn their heads, mine left, yours right.

That evening is a fact.
I am still here in its field.

May Tenth

Ten on May tenth,
you think it's fine:
two numbers in your age
till you're a hundred.

You've learned to flip
your silky hair in such a way
your unsure eyes don't show.
Your unruly arms and legs
most often seem askew,
but you can still curl up
like a touched caterpillar
and suck your thumb.

Ten years ago this hour
you uncurled from me.
Weak and silly from ether and relief,
I took you
into the crook of my arm,
felt the rush of blood
that cleared the blurring gas.

Satisfied,
I kissed the spot on your bare head
that throbbed.

Stoney Creek That Afternoon

If she was there
it was the way light falls
through turning leaves,
in slants and shafts across the path,
in circles of October light
balanced over streaming water.

It is not clear that he was ever there.
Unless like silver birch leaves parting
to let light in, golden locust
closing at the whim of wind, still
warm enough to be a breeze.
Or maybe he was light, she the valving leaves.

The Party

The Party

It's an old story, what happens later.
How dark the dance is, how loud, how drunk.
Talking is shouting, touching a joke.
Shadows of solo dancers writhe like snakes
up the walls of the barn to the rafters
and sink down again when the music breaks,
and rise and fall, and rise and fall in the smoke.

The Adamsons' Peacocks

Brakes screech, heavy metal thunks. A second, then glass crashes.
Behind my woods there's been another wreck on Three Chopt Road.

Waiting for the sirens makes me hear the silence,
And in that silence come uncanny human cries for help.

I've lived here long enough to know this cry
Is like, but only like, a woman's in the labor room,

Or a woman slammed against a wall with two hands on her shoulders
Who knows that what those hands do next will kill her in some way.

Help, oh, help, oh, help: the desperate aspirants of pain,
The long vowels of howling the long hours of the first birth.

Or the cry you tried to stifle, trying to be quiet, to hide
From someone—the parents, the children—the truest sound you make.

The way a peacock calls its mate: unseemly, raucous, screamed.
Like brakes too late, like any passion over the limit,

Beyond the gorgeous plumage, after the measured dancing,
Past any sequential ritual we ever learned.

Seasons

Sunburned, you cast across the surf
off Hatteras, reeling in the blues.
Your deft flicks—I wanted to kiss
the tendons in your wrist.

At night we fried the fish in butter.
Your body was so beautiful, so hot
and briny to my tongue.

By dove season the sun still burned
in the stubbled fields.
We unpacked the pouch of your sweaty vest,
sat on stools ripping handfuls of feathers
from the warm birds. Our kitchen thickened
with gray down that rose like smoke
around us.

When it was cold enough for geese
you couldn't go. You pressed my palm
against your chest and cried. It's barbed,
you said, this hook in here.
The surgeon's word was *riddled*.

The cedar leans from its tricky stand.
I've pricked my finger stringing berries,
rub my eyes against my wrist.
Tommy struggles with the tangled lights—
Goddamn, he says in the voice that wants
to be yours.
Hush, I warn. But I know you
don't hear from upstairs.

You're moving slowly through snow
over Roanoke Ridge
holding the shotgun
before you with both hands.
The berry-fat grouse drums once from the hemlock.
You raise your gun, his wings lift for flight.

Power Failure

All the relations sleep.

Forced to early beds by lack of light
Mother, sister, husband, children
have left me
cat-eyed
to delight in my own power.

The storm that downed the wires is over,
steady rain's moved into the backyard.

I sit on the top of the steps,
bare feet getting rained on,
watching the lightning bug
high in the pin oak
bright as the end of my cigarette.
Below me a gardenia glows
unconnected to its charcoal foliage.

A gray shape shifts among these
blacks and lights.
Another cat does not surprise me.

Leaning against the screen door
I'm vanishing with a Cheshire smile.
For not one of them—
Mother, sister, husband, children—
will travel the black house sightless,
come up behind me,
see what I am up to

until the power comes back on.

At the Edge

At the edge of our house
that wedges the curve of yard

I lie in the curling breeze
swing in a net of rope.

The slate roof angles into sky,
gray slate piercing moon-black.

I move in gentle arcs
while your heart beats
in sleep inside
our hard house.

I sway, awake to slate and edge,
soft in the midnight air.

Ways We Come Apart

"At the seams" suggests a remedy:
a stitch in time might save us.

Growing apart is sadder, so slow,
so gradual it can slip your attention
the way the Earth never jerks itself out
from under your feet, yet moves,
is moving right now, away from where
you think it stands.

Falling apart can appear to be
a pair of skydivers
waving across the air.
Or you can hear it: the clunk of parts
and bolts shearing off a junkyard car.

But that's not true enough
to what I know you mean.

It's not just in your head
where your thoughts skip and drop
like rocks in a slide. But the satellite's
fragments are due in our streets.
Your mother fell and cracked her hip.
Your husband's dark eyes split
into glittering shards.

As you tell me why,
you knock my glass off the table,
stand there crying like a girl
over pieces at your feet.

The Settlement

It was so silent
after my raucous children
had scrambled into their father's car
and his tires ground out the gravel drive,
I leaned for a moment
against the screen door, waiting
for small breaking sounds
like those that crack the quiet
of winter woods.

Nothing snapped. A warm breeze
carried the call of mourning doves
across the yard, the rising notes
of someone calling Celia in to dinner.

I walked out over the new grass
to the white azaleas tall as I am,
plunged my hands through the blossoms
into the woody interior, grasped
two branches brittle as old wrists
and broke them.

Walking back to the house I held
the hundred flowers against my breast.

Caravati's Junkyard

Dried sinks and hot
iceboxes squat on
the chickweed.
Fireless mantels
gape from a shed.

Doors without houses
lean still and stiff
on Caravati's fence.
Doors without handles
unhinged in the sun
peel to their
useful wood.

Beyond stacks of
banisters, past
piles of wrought
iron railings,
in an empty
ragweed lot,
one door stands up

closing on Caravati's
Junkyard, opening
on goldenrod,
hinging on air.

Fall Jazz

Wynton Marsalis' trumpet called down the walls
at the concert, and I'm driving home with a sound
in my head like another country's siren. Stopped
at the tollgate I toss in my quarter and wait
for the flimsy barrier to shudder and lift.

Vapor-lit lanes of the Downtown Expressway double
at the bright row of tollbooths, then narrow
to thread the underpass, emerge alongside the wall
of the Spring Street Prison, where the lights
in an acre of windows have been put out for the night.

Marsalis' horn in the coliseum could have swept
the city like the beam of a truck-mounted searchlight
and found the cell of the man who stared down
at his enormous hands when I rose and said
We find the defendant guilty, Your Honor.

Guilty of attempting to break out of Spring Street
with a weapon he fashioned from pieces of sink
he'd wrenched from the concrete wall with his hands.
By tonight he'd be back on his bunk and aware
of the passage of traffic on the Downtown Expressway.

And the intermittent wail of a trumpet's sweep.
He cups one curved hand over a fist in front
of his lips and blows on his thumb,
fingering the stops of air. He's alone,
I know, because that's what we sentenced him to.

At home, I let myself in through the kitchen,
click on the floodlight and lean toward the window
over my sink. Out there the crickets insist
like jazz. The last chrysanthemums stand back
by the fence, violet at the edge of the light.

January Flies

Such moist warmth, such insistent
rhythm must have spawned them—
the furnace basso harrumphing off, on, off
on against these zero nights, the laundry's
hot wet water, hot dry air, cycle on cycle,
steam fuzzing up the walls like lush mold—
a fly could hardly resist being born.

When I opened the basement door I gasped
and slammed it on a scene from a disaster flick:
a swarm of fat black flies bobbing up the stairway
toward my face.

Since then I'm bent on annihilation,
gassings through the cracked door. For three
who made it through I raised a window,
watched them drone to a freedom
where the garbage is frozen. I found one
floating, glistening black in my son's milk.

Tonight there's one more left. The fittest,
I suppose, has made it up another flight, survives
in my bedroom. This fly is delirious.
With death, I don't know, with the perfume
in my room? With some sense the time's all wrong?

It flings its fizzing blood against the windowpane
and I come at it with a rolled magazine, inflamed
out of proportion, vertiginous as a January fly.

Stillness Like This

It's stillness that gets you,
not a dingy Greyhound leaving at dawn,
grinding to somewhere strange.
But sit very still in a familiar diner,
expect no one.
Such times you'll feel like a building.

Even leaving you was motion—
your car, then
three airports, two planes, a taxi.
The pilot pointed out Manhattan, Ellis Island.
When we passengers leaned together to look,
the plane tipped to the left. And flying
low over Maryland it cast a shadow
sharp as a sparrow hawk cruising the cornfield.

But what gets you is stillness like this,
lying awake before birds sing to light.
No one is breathing in this house except me.
Out at the curb my car is parked in stone.

Safeway

This world is category. Raw meat
In slick clear film does not insinuate
Its bloody flesh into meringue-topped sweet
Potato pie. Dark beer and milk don't mate
In this geometry. The Safeway's grid
Defines my need: aisle B the bread, white wine
On C, detergent stacked to pyramid.
The orange and onion never cross their line.
So how come this crippled child bisects my path?
Careens his wheelchair, jerks his body. Why
Does he cock his heavy head at me and laugh
With such strange glee? I can't meet his eye.
I came to this sane place to be alone,
To choose my food, to buy it, to go home.

A Friend of Hopkins

One night in my kitchen you cried out THE DARK!
and stared somewhere, I held your hands hard
and begged tell me, can't you tell me, this
darkness, tell me what it's like, but you
jerked your hands away and hid your face
It is a place is all you said Oh the mind
the mind has cliffs Can I fix you a drink?
You shook your head still holding it on or
trying to wring out the dark, Cliffs of fall
frightful, sheer, Should I call a doctor?
Do you want to spend the night in my bed?
Please, please tell me what I can do. You
lowered your hands and looked at me with
scorn: You've never hung here you said.

Volcanic

Like night coming on the wrong way
the cinder cloud from Mount St. Helens
crosses the continent from West to East.

Earth turns backward and today, here
in Virginia, it seems earlier
than anywhere else in the country.

At noon the lake reflects our fishing poles.
The sunstruck dragonflies couple and hum.
When you say we're getting younger every minute
your eyes are as clear as this air.

Even so, Montana is dark.
Twilight is coming to Kansas,
shadow to the Appalachians.
Before long I'll look at your bare shoulders
and see the fine ash there.
And my hand, reaching to you, gloved in dust.

Tidewater Climbing Company

Lures me from sea level.
They've set up shop above the oyster bar
(with not even a hill on our horizon)
to outfit us with the gear
it takes to live on the vertical.

The store is newly rustic, windowless.
Its clean dust floats in gaslight
to floors of unfinished pine.

People in posters wear jackets sold here
filled with down
Their cleated boots are planted
in cliffsides, their bright bodies jut
like prows into deep blue air.

What it takes to poise them there
is here. Even my mouth fills up
with the sense of small clunky steel:
couplings, grapples, little pulleys.

Strange hardware tips my inner ear.

My fingers search for purchase
on more familiar textures—
hemp and canvas, coiled cord
wound on wooden spools.

I feel the tug of this good rope
guying my swimming body to rock,
holding me to surfaces
when I would sink.

I take a breath,
push from the edge
of the splintered counter,
rappel out the door—
or am I diving?—
down the pineboard steps
to the flat, sea-smelling street.

The Luncheon of the Boating Party

Heron

The moment between what wasn't
and what is
has to shock like the instant
I saw the three-foot heron
perched like a prank
in my front yard.

I've known a few annunciations.
My God I'm in love was one,
and the bloodied baby's head
between my thighs. Then
my thin son with a suitcase,
losing resolution
in my rearview mirror.

The elegant heron stood in my yard,
in my cluttered neighborhood,
miles from water, fish, its kind.
It curled and uncurled its neck,
scanning the air for bearings.

All morning I thought
it would fly away.
By afternoon I was afraid
it never would.

Who could miss this incongruous sight?
Everyone who passed by did.
Walkers, drivers, runners, children
never noticed the great blue heron
dying by my Pontiac.

It stood there all day long,
bearing its weight
on legs as frail as marsh grass.

Beyond Recognition

A lesion that destroys this area of the cerebral
cortex impairs the ability to identify a person by
facial features.
—*Scientific American*

And though there is no sudden face
in the doorway that makes you rush
to touch its familiar cheek,
neither is there the face
that causes you to cringe
or triggers the wish to smash it.

The leering face in the kitchen window
you couldn't erase from dreams
since you were eight,
the face you never could unmask
yet live with on a vow,
the wrinkled woman in your mirror

are innocent of history
as this problem child who comes to visit.

You ask me every time
in that same expectant voice

Now who are you?

All My Friends' Pets Are Growing Old

All my friends' pets are growing old.
Mike's clawless, scabby cat can't roam outside
for fear the bluejays she once mocked will strike
and peck her sores. So Mike picks up the turds
from his prize rugs with only mild disgust
and smiles at Tiger sleeping in a shaft of sun.
Barbara said at lunch the other day she's lugging
her black Lab (with help to push him up
into the car) weekly to the vet's for shots
and every Tuesday he plays dead at two o'clock.
I thought how much I'd hate a week with such a time
tied to it. I didn't like her dog when
he was frisky. I did like Millie's Corgi
who looked old when he was new, but I hate
the way she talks now of his cancer
as if he were a relative or friend.
Bob and Connie Kincaid are the worst
with their menagerie—a house that reeks of cat
piss, two huge wheezing dogs, and one with heart-
worm, a hamster worn to lumpenness from running round
in circles, a toothless rabbit, Aphrodite,
they coax to suck a bottle. And talk,
that's all they do is talk of all the trouble
they go to, so smug the way they're trying to
suggest they'd do the same for anyone. And the part
I really cannot bear, they trick me
into talking about Whitlock Street, where
we couples stood around somebody's small backyard,
grilling sirloins, sipping beer, a nudge or hug
to go with watching Millie's puppy waddle
grass-high toward the plump legs of our diapered babies.

Halloween

I. Stuart Circle Hospital

They gave me no choice, dried
my milk with a shot, tried
to make me sleep.

But I lie here and watch the light fall
through gingko and maple, the last
of the fans and the golden stars
brushing Jeb Stuart, settling
on the brim of his bronze plumed hat.

On this last afternoon in October
the piles of leaves on Stuart Circle
are high enough to hide a child,
and I see one yellow mound erupt
in fans and stars and arms
of a monster who yells "trick or treat."

Somewhere they swaddle my newborn son
in gauze and plaster, try to straighten
the bones that bent inside my womb.

It's almost dark when they bring him to me,
the plaster still warm.
The casts turn cold as I hold him
against my stone breast

while children clatter on cobblestones,
circling General Stuart
in their dimestore disguises.

II. In the Nursery

Locked into knotted bone
by a flawed code
you were born
like the black child
with evil connotations.

40

Like the snake
whose beauty can't compensate:
he will never play it straight.

Nothing straight about you.
Under the baby skin
you're gnarled as a sinister tree.
You'll walk if at all
with the awkward crab.

You share words that describe
with the crooked man,
the twisted mind,
the warped, the wicked.

Oh who can ever straighten you out?

A cramped fist to God for crippled things,
for all things clotted and kinked.

I look at you
and my own dark knots can't be undone.

III. A Birthday

Legs braced in metal,
a pillowcase ghost,
you kick the new ball
fall laughing
into the pile of maple leaves.

Your brown eyes shine
with points of light
like the jack-o'-lantern's
we just lit.

Your sister pulls you up,
your brother ties helium balloons
to your useless wrists.

For one frozen moment I'm certain
you'll rise and float away.

Let go, let go
you have to say
before I even know
I have pinned your golden head
to my heart.

Red

One red poppy wild in the brush,
this cracked clay pot of fluttering poppies,
stays the gray, the ash, the beige
of that field, this end of town.

This cracked clay pot of fluttering poppies
a woman raised from seed
of that field. This end of town
holds no other brightness.

A woman raised from seed
everything red; the flesh
holds no other brightness.
Skins are shades of beige.

Everything red, the flesh,
fields, tenements, oceans try to conceal.
Skins are shades of beige,
skies are darknesses.

Fields, tenements, oceans try to conceal
the alarming life of red.
Skies are darknesses
the ambulance sun runs through.

The alarming life of red
spills from the body.
The ambulance sun runs through—
dangerous/vital/dangerous/vital.

Spills from the body,
one red poppy wild in the brush—
dangerous/vital/dangerous/vital—
stays the gray, the ash, the beige.

Neighborhood

I jerk awake at dawn to snarls.
Guttural, dangerous. In my yard
three dogs are tearing up my cat.

They stretch her to three points above the grass,
bend their necks between their stiff front legs,
stake her with their teeth.

I charge out in my nightgown,
wave my bare arms as if I held weapons.

Or no, I just think so. Motionless
I stand at the window and watch them finish.

Two lope off across my lawn and down the street.
The third trots home next door
where the family calls him Caleb.

They've trained him to come when they whistle,
to leap and catch sticks in midair.

Waiting for You

Tiger, when I was fleet
and could leap and sprint
a hundred miles an hour
you never lifted your lazy eyes
or your shaggy head above the grasses.

Now my haunch leaks drops of blood
on the blades you'll move through.

My pores taint the air
to lead you my lame way.

I know
before you do
that I am trapped in your stalking.

Your eyes will bead
on the clues of my wound.
Your nostrils will tighten around my smell.
You will rise and stripe
the yellow grass.

Tiger, you'll move with the stride of a tyrant.
Slowly, toward a sure thing.

Counting Sheep

The drunk in the kitchen is Mother.
The dry metal *crack* is the ice tray.
The long liquid silence is whiskey.
The spigot's quick gush is the water.
The cupboard doors banging is searching.
The one-sided talking is pleading.
The God-damning sobbing is praying.
The dry metal *crack* is the ice tray.
The drunk in the kitchen is Mother.

Her Words

Mother wrote words
on the torn-off margins of magazines,
then she held each scrap
to the flame of her lighter.

Writing and burning,
drinking bourbon,
she sat all night at the counter
writing and burning in the fluorescent kitchen.

One morning I turned off the light
and claimed two black-edged fragments
from the ashtray. One said sham, the other Go.
Maybe shame or God, or maybe not.

When I asked, she shrugged
and never left another sign.
In daylight I find the glass
ashtray racked with the dishes.

Mother stands at the stove, stirring soup,
her glasses opaque with steam.
She talks about nothing
that makes any difference.

When she wipes her glasses and turns
to me, her eyes are edged with ashes.
She looks straight through the light
naming something that I cannot see.

The Pathos of the Inadequate

Mother called from the hospital,
woke me at five, whispering
my nickname as a question:
Buff?

Every ring that week had wrecked me
but to hear her voice come from the dead
of my sleep burst my voice from its cords
like a scream: Mother!
She had been beyond speech for three days.
Mother. What is it?

And another thing, Buffy,
she said in her long-gone
tone for instruction, run
down to the basement. Look
in the largest hanging bag. Find
my black Dior jacket. And take
it with you. Go now
she demanded. I'll wait.

But I don't—I began,
well, O.K., sure. You know I love
your black Dior jacket. Hang on, Mama.
Then nestled the telephone into my pillow
and ran.

Locking Up

In '54 a bunch of boys slipped through the pines
to my ground-floor bedroom, stuck a goose through
the loose screen. "What in God's name!" exclaimed
Mother when we heard the honks from the kitchen.

"Boys!" she'd laugh, as if that flapping gander
were a valentine to both of us.

When I lived there you never knew
who'd come through the warped french doors—
the starting five from Northside High
teasing Mother for a beer; Daddy's laughing
Belgian cousins; Ginny, Mother's friend who'd walk
right in my bathroom and ask for some shampoo.

Now those doors are planed and sanded to take the deadbolt
locks; each pane is framed by wire that sets off sirens.
After two robberies Mother said she felt violated.

After her funeral I woke up dry and cold
back in my old room, my throat and eyelids scratched
by air conditioning. I tried to raise the windows
for the humid Georgia air, but every frame was fitted
with a lock that took a key.

It's the only thing, I guess, we know to do with fear,
and not enough. Here, though I lock up early,
as soon as it gets dark, the face appears
in my kitchen window and even if I pull the shade
I can't keep out the words I saw it mouthing:

I've found the way past all your Mother's locks,
I'll find the way past yours.

Vision

Is this the check?
For all the things I gave other names,
for the fun of changing things to suit me,
for naming things I never saw

a mailbox becomes a woman bent
dangerously close to the highway—
and I'm honking at a mailbox like a fool.

Today I read *infinite*
instead of *infertile* to my class
and they laughed.

Especially at dusk
when I need something, or someone,
things disappear.

At intersections trucks turn gray,
evaporate. Is this the charge
for two-ton realities
I failed to see,
so set on looking?

The big things blur
like (here I go again) Casco Bay
the night the fog absorbed the Broadway lights
of the Nova Scotia cruise ship.

When it passed my dock I only knew
I was staring right at it
when I heard band music, and people singing.

U.F.O. Off the Coast of Maine

You jump up, try to pull me away.
It's frightening, something I've never seen,
can't fit with any name.

Is it something coming to get us?

But what if that sourceless beam of light
aimed straight at the rock we sit on is
something coming
to take us right now, together, out of this world?

This has been a day that burst into our tent
from the Atlantic, the sun splintering mica
off of the rocks, out of the grayest wave.

Morning of woodsmoke, then our gradually warming
skin. We unlayered ourselves to July—
sweaters, then flannels, then everything
except our hands on each other.

In the last violet light we layered ourselves
again, sat in the grass drinking cold beer.
When the stars came out
we walked down here to sit on this flat rock.

I'm old enough to guess how many days like this are left.

As this unearthly light moves closer
I'd just as soon stay still.
Come here. Come sit back down beside me.

Translations

For Mimi and Susan, translators

Borges thinks.

Through his library window in Argentina
the late southern light moves
warmly on his hand.

The warmth takes shape, form, contrast,
light and dark in motion, then:
tigers, rivers.

He sees inside his head
as we all do.
But it is not enough.

Science tells us why
we can't be content
with these wonders in our heads:

we must know, yet can be certain
of nothing, can hold on to nothing
that moves in time.

So Borges speaks
the Spanish names
for what he sees.

He arranges, rearranges them in air
until their sequence is magic
and tigers, rivers move
but do not change.

At the desk, his mother
who is ninety-five
sets down the symbols for his words.

For eyes as blind to Spanish
symbols as his own,
Borges' river is redrawn,

bursts through the English
into the eyes of a girl reading
in a fluorescent American library.

The river writhes like tigers
and will not be still until
she tells it to someone else.

Read this man Borges
she writes to an artist,
who reads, and sees.

The rush of the river
cannot be dammed.
It flows through her fingers
back to white paper.

Now, far from Argentina
the same sun shafts
through my library window
on the drawing the artist gave me.

It is a river,
a river striped with light and dark
that churns and stalks the white
yet is unmoved by time.

I stand before it
and behind my eyes—
my eyes—

Borges thinks.

Luncheon of the Boating Party

Long before he had to strap the brushes
to his wrists, Renoir had stolen time.
He'd learned a way to preserve afternoons,
glint sun on crystal by laying on pure white,
distill white wine with dabs of ocher.
And a thick black line can set an awning flapping.

It's true that falling sun lights crystal.
Under Catherine's awning in Indian summer
the rosehips glow against the low brick wall.
I preserve them, she says, reaching behind her
languidly to pick one. Paul's bare forearm rests
on the tablecloth. My fingers uncurl
from the stem of the wineglass and spread
until my little finger touches the fine hair
on his wrist. A crumpled napkin lies between
the empty emerald bottle and the amber one.

Renoir posed his brawny friends in sleeveless shirts,
used blue to bulge the muscles in their upper arms.
For him the girl he loved held still
until the sun was right, on her rounded cheek,
on Brett's straw hat, on the folds of white linen.

William knuckles the ears of his arching cat, tells
one last summer story. Our laughter's as low
as the rumbling purr, as the breeze fluttering
the scalloped awning. Paul is watching Catherine
crush the rosehip. William's smiling drowsily at me.

And yet, at forty-one, Renoir disdained this painting
and all his other art. "I have forgotten,"
he wrote to Brett, "how either to paint or to draw,"
and in 1882 he left for Rome to study the frescoes
of Raphael. Critics today prefer his late work,
its more formal concerns, its rich paint. In the last
pictures the human body becomes almost abstract.